COLUMBIA SLAVIC STUDIES

A SERIES OF THE
DEPARTMENT OF SLAVIC LANGUAGES, COLUMBIA UNIVERSITY
ERNEST J. SIMMONS, GENERAL EDITOR

SLAVIC LANGUAGES

A CONDENSED SURVEY

BY

ROMAN JAKOBSON

HARVARD UNIVERSITY

Second Edition

KING'S CROWN PRESS

NEW YORK AND LONDON

The preparation and publication of the several series of works under SLAVIC STUDIES have been made possible by a grant from the Rockefeller Foundation to the Department of Slavic Languages of Columbia University.

ERNEST J. SIMMONS
EXECUTIVE OFFICER

KING'S CROWN PRESS

is an imprint established by Columbia University Press for the purpose of making certain scholarly material available at minimum cost. Toward that end, the publishers have used standardized formats incorporating every reasonable economy that does not interfere with legibility. The author has assumed complete responsibility for editorial style and for proofreading.

SECOND EDITION 1955

First printing 1955
Second printing 1963

LIBRARY OF CONGRESS CATALOG CARD NUMBER: 55-7389

PRINTED IN THE UNITED STATES OF AMERICA

CONTENTS

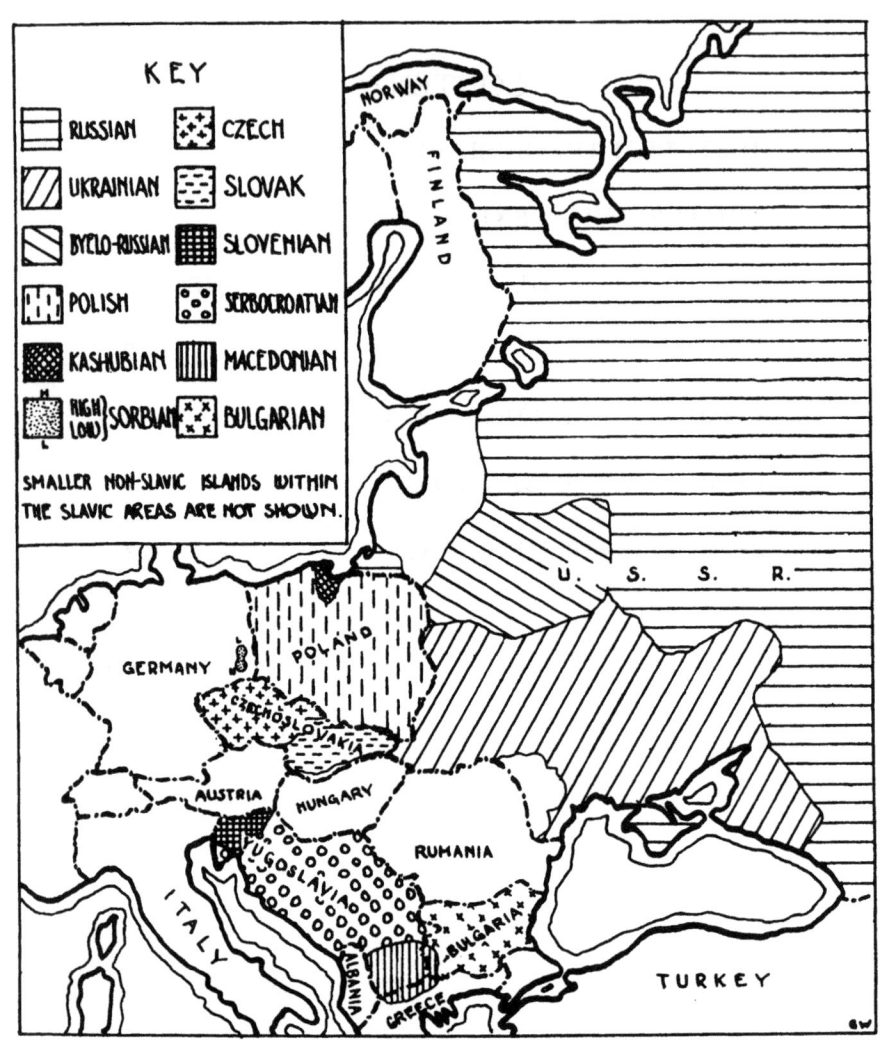

KEY

RUSSIAN	CZECH
UKRAINIAN	SLOVAK
BYELO-RUSSIAN	SLOVENIAN
POLISH	SERBOCROATIAN
KASHUBIAN	MACEDONIAN
HIGH LOW SORBIAN	BULGARIAN

SMALLER NON-SLAVIC ISLANDS WITHIN
THE SLAVIC AREAS ARE NOT SHOWN.

APPROXIMATE DISTRIBUTION OF SLAVIC
LANGUAGES IN PRESENT-DAY EUROPE

MAP PREPARED BY G. WEINREICH

DISTRIBUTION, SUBDIVISIONS

AT THE PRESENT TIME the Slavic world comprises thirteen languages, each with a distinct literary standard. In the usual classification they are distributed into three groups—Eastern, Western, and Southern Slavic.

Eastern Slavs. (1) RUSSIAN (Great-Russian) is spoken as a native language by the preponderant majority (73 per cent) in the Russian SFSR and by minor groups in the other Republics of the Union of Soviet Socialist Republics. Moreover, being the principal cultural and state language of the USSR, it is employed as a second tongue in nearly all parts of the Soviet Union that have non-Russian native populations. The study of Russian is promoted on a vast scale in the school programs of all, especially Slavic, states within the Soviet sphere of influence; the official Soviet phraseology labels Russian as "the future world language of Socialism." (2) UKRAINIAN (Little-Russian, Ruthenian) is the native language of the vast majority in the Ukrainian SSR and of minor groups in the RSFSR and some other Republics of the Soviet Union. Outside the USSR, there is a compact Ukrainian minority in Northeastern Slovakia. (3) BYELO-RUSSIAN (White-Russian, White-Ruthenian) is the major language of the Byelo-Russian SSR. According to official Soviet estimates, at the start of the Second World War there were in the Eastern Hemisphere some 99 million native speakers of Russian, over 36 million of Ukrainian, and up to 8 million of Byelo-Russian.

Western Slavs. (4) POLISH is the native tongue of the overwhelming majority of the present population of Poland, of 100,000 Poles in the Těšín district of Czechoslovakia, and of a vanishing minority in those parts of pre-War Poland incorporated into the USSR; in all, at least 21 million speak Polish in the Eastern Hemisphere. (5) KASHUBIAN is spoken in Poland by some

1

200,000 people on the left bank of the Lower Vistula. To the northwest, away from this compact Kashubian area (in the Stołp district), survive the last few families that still know SLOVINCIAN, an archaic variant of Kashubian. These are the remnants of the POMORANIAN group which in the early Middle Ages extended from the Lower Vistula to the Lower Oder and was later Germanized. The Pomoranian group together with Polish belongs to the larger unit of the so-called LEKHITIC languages, which also includes POLABIAN, the former language of the Elbe (Laba) area. The last remnant of Polabian on the left bank of the lower Elbe (Dravāno-Polabian) died out toward the middle of the eighteenth century, but is known through a few vocabulary lists and short texts recorded about 1700. The other extinct Lekhitic languages are known only from isolated words and proper names, mostly toponymic. The Kashubs were alternately under Polish and German rule and thus were subjected both to a heavy Germanization and to a strong influence of the closely related Polish language. At the present time Kashubian is treated as a regional vernacular, and its cultural role is limited to a few folk publications, plays, radio programs, and social gatherings. (6) and (7) LOW and HIGH SORBIAN (Lusatian, Lower and Upper Wendish) are spoken by some 150,000 people on the Upper Spree. Surrounded by German, they form two neighboring linguistic islets, the northern one being Low Lusatia (Dolna Lužica) in Prussia and the adjacent part of Saxony with its center at Kottbus (Chośebuz), and the southern one being Upper Lusatia (Hornja Lužica) in Saxony with its center at Bautzen (Budyšin)—the former Protestant and the latter Catholic. Together with the disappearing Eastern Sorbian dialect around Muskau (Mužakow), these are the last remnants of a linguistic group that was quite extensive during the Middle Ages and bordered Polabian on the North, Polish on the East, and Czech on the South, forming a linguistically intermediate zone between these three languages. After the Second World War both Sorbian languages have been, for the first time, introduced into primary and secondary schools of Lusatia. (8) CZECH is, since the postwar transfer of the German minority, almost the only language of the whole western part of Czechoslovakia (Bohemia

2

and Moravia including the Czech part of old Silesia). Adjacent to this compact area, there are small Czech communities in Kladsko and Upper Silesia (both belonging to present-day Poland). (9) SLOVAK is the predominant native language of Slovakia (an autonomous part of Czechoslovakia). In Europe Czech is spoken by over 8½ million and Slovak about 3 million people.

Southern Slavs. (10) SLOVENIAN is spoken in the Slovenian People's Republic (an autonomous unit within Yugoslovia) and in small adjacent areas of Austria and Italy. (11) SERBO-CROATIAN covers the greatest part of Yugoslavia: Serbia, Montenegro, Bosnia-Herzegovina, and Croatia. In the Europe of 1940 Slovenian was spoken by almost 1¾ million and Serbocroatian by some 11 million people. The standard language of the Greek Orthodox Serbs and the Catholic Croats is the same, except for a few lexical variations and the adaptation of the Russian alphabet by the former and of the Latin by the latter. (12) MACEDONIAN is the prevailing language of the Macedonian People's Republic (an autonomous unit within Yugoslavia). The central dialect, belonging to the Western Macedonian group, has recently been elevated to the status of a standard language. There are about a million native Macedonians including those in the adjacent areas of Bulgaria and Greece. (13) BULGARIAN is the dominant language in Bulgaria. At the end of 1940 it was spoken by about 6 million people in Europe including Bulgarian colonies in the USSR and Bulgars in the part of Dobrudja that remained under Rumania.

Incomplete data on the extent of some of the Slavic languages in the United States are given in the 1940 census: 585,080 people with Russian as their mother-tongue; 83,000 (?) with Ukrainian; 2,416,320 with Polish; 520,440 with Czech; 484,360 with Slovak; 178,640 with Slovenian; 153,080 with Serbocroatian. From the Canadian census of 1951 we may cite the following figures indicating the mother tongue: Ukrainian, 352,323; Polish, 129,238; Slovak, 45,516; Russian, 39,223; Serbocroatian, 11,031.

As a consequence of World War II, western Byelo-Russia was detached from Poland, and the western Ukrainian areas from Poland, Czechoslovakia, and Rumania and were incorporated into the USSR; the Polish and Kashubian sections of Germany passed to Poland; some Slovenian and Croatian dominions of Italy to Yugoslavia; and a part of Dobrudja was returned from Rumania to Bulgaria. The total number of Slavs in the world is now over 200 million. Except for a few border minorities and Americans with Slavic mother-tongues, all Slavic peoples, save the Sorbs, live in states with a Slavic majority and state language—USSR, Poland, Czechoslovakia, Yugoslavia, and Bulgaria.

Between the three Eastern Slavic languages there are intermediate dialectal areas. Russian is divided into Northern, Southern and transitional (Middle Russian) dialects, each of them with archaic islets presenting salient common features. Ukrainian dialects are classified into Northern, Southeastern, Southwestern, and Carpathian groups; the marginal dialects (called Rusnak) of the latter group are Slovak-influenced. Byelo-Russian is divided into two dialects—the Northeastern and the Southwestern, disclosing a stronger Polish impact. Polish contains, besides various border dialects, two fundamental groups: Great and Little Polish in the Northwest and Southeast respectively. Kashubian comprehends two types of dialects: the Southern, and the Northern, which includes Slovincian. In Czech there are Bohemian, Central Moravian, and Silesian groups, with transitional dialects from group to group and from Czech to Slovak and to Polish. Slovak consists of three dialectal types: Central; Western, closely linked with Czech; and Eastern, connected with Polish and Ukrainian. Slovenian exhibits great dialectal variety. Serbocroatian from East to West presents three basic groups: Štokavian, Čakavian, and Kajkavian which is transitional to Slovenian. Bulgarian is divided into three basic dialects: Western, Northeastern, and Southeastern. Macedonian sets up a scale of intermediary dialectal zones between West Bulgarian and Štokavian.

PROTOSLAVIC; EXPANSION

PROTOSLAVIC (Primitive Slavic), which substituted (1) s, z for advanced k, g, and (2) x for the old s preceded by i, u, r, k, was a Western offshoot of the satem-group of Indo-European languages and shares the fusion of *a* and *o* with the majority of this group. Common isoglosses testify a close and prolonged neighborhood with Germanic, Iranian, probably Thraco-Phrygian and foremost with Baltic, which is tied to Slavic by significant innovations both in vocabulary and in grammatical and phonemic, especially prosodic, features. Old loan-words from Iranian pertain mostly to spiritual, and those from Germanic to material culture. Contact with Altaic and Finno-Ugric languages seems to be confined to the late stage of Protoslavic and has left but scanty vestiges in its vocabulary. The long evolution of Protoslavic, which took around three millennia, can be traced up to its final stage—the entrance of the Slavs onto the historical scene (fifth–sixth centuries), the oldest foreign records of Slavic proper and common nouns (fifth–seventh centuries), the formation of the first hereditary Slavic states (ninth–tenth centuries), the appearance of Slavic written literature (ninth century), and the final dissolution of the Slavic linguistic unity toward the beginning of our millennium.

The territory of present-day Poland, Byelo-Russia, and North-western Ukraine seems to exhibit perceptible vestiges of the oldest Slavic settlements. According to the first detailed literary accounts about the Slavs, the sixth century A.D. witnessed a strong Slavic expansion to the South, West, and East. The Slavs swarmed over the Peloponnesos during the seventh century, but were eventually driven back from Greece. With Charlemagne began the protracted retreat of the Slavs in the West and the gradual Germanization of the Elbe and Oder basins in the Northwest and of the Slavic regions of Bavaria and Austria in the Southwest. In the tenth century the Southern Slavs became separated from the Western because of this continuous German offensive toward and the Hungarian intrusion from the East; later they were cut off also from the Eastern Slavs by the extension of Rumanian. While the expansion of the Western and Southern Slavs was curtailed and even repelled during the early Middle Ages, that of the Eastern Slavs has never stopped and particularly their colonization of the East still continued, checked only in the Bering Sea area in the late nineteenth century.

5

HISTORY OF THE LITERARY
LANGUAGES

SLAVIC LITERARY ACTIVITIES begin in the ninth century with the rise of the first Slavic national state, Great Moravia, where two Byzantine missionaries brought up in Macedonia (Salonika), St. Cyril (Constantine the Philosopher, an erudite polyglot, formerly professor at the University of Constantinople) and his brother, St. Methodius, organized in the 'sixties a national church with services in Slavic. For this purpose they translated the Bible, liturgic and other ecclesiastic texts into the Slavic dialect spoken in the Salonika region, patterning it after the Greek model and adapting it to the Czechoslovak linguistic habits of Great Moravia. Since the dialectal differentiation of the primitive Slavic language at that time was insignificant, there were no obstacles for the spread of this Macedonian vernacular among the great majority of the Slavs as their first written and liturgic language. The literary activities of the two Slavic apostles were preceded only by a few primary Christian texts (such as the Baptismal Vows, the Paternoster, Credo, etc.) translated probably in Great Moravia in the early ninth century, partly from Latin, partly perhaps from Old High German, and preserved in later copies. The Moravian mission was forcibly terminated in 885, after some two decades of work, but it had given the Slavs many standard translations from Greek and occasionally from Latin, as well as original homilies, legends, prayers, and poems in a new but highly elaborate literary language adaptable for scholarly and poetic expression. Moreover, it bequeathed to them the lasting idea of the propriety and the necessity of using the mother tongue for all, even the highest, cultural purposes. This literary language, called by modern scholars OLD CHURCH SLAVONIC (Old Slavic, or inaccurately Old Bulgarian), penetrated from the late ninth to the eleventh centuries into the whole Slavic world except for its Northwestern margin. It produced several local variants: the MORAVIAN recension itself is known to us only indirectly through later copies made in other areas, the BOHEMIAN recension, which exhibits Latin influence, is preserved as far as indigenous manuscripts

6

are concerned, in single fragments of the tenth and eleventh centuries, and moreover local literary activities are known through some later foreign, mostly Russian, copies; the MACEDONIAN recension, particularly conservative in its vocabulary and phraseology; the BULGARIAN recension, which weeded out Greek and Moravian words and expressions, created a new rich terminology, and reflected the intense scholarly and literary life of Bulgaria in the early tenth century—these last two recensions are preserved in several manuscripts of the eleventh century and in many later copies; the CROATIAN and SERBIAN recensions, both manifesting a strong Macedonian influence and attested by twelfth century manuscripts; and the Eastern Slavic (usually called RUSSIAN) recension offering the oldest of the dated Slavic manuscripts preserved, Ostromir's Evangelium (written in 1056), as well as some twenty-five Kiev and Novgorod manuscripts of the eleventh century and numerous others of later date—copies of Southern and Western Slavic originals, and in a great part, local creations. This recension derived from the Bulgarian but later tended rather toward the Macedonian and in its further development has shown a repeated reciprocity with the Serbian recension. The Freising Fragments of the late tenth century in Latin letters seem to be a SLOVENIAN modification of Old Church Slavonic. During the twelfth century the language of Cyril and Methodius, wherever it appears in the Slavic world, is essentially modified; the Old Church Slavonic period ends and thenceforth we speak simply of CHURCH SLAVONIC.

With the Great Schism of 1054 and the First Crusade, Latin triumphed as the only liturgic and literary language for all of the Western Slavs and for the Western part of the South Slavic area. Of the Catholic Slavic peoples, only a part of the Croats preserved the use of Church Slavonic in liturgy and literature and spread this use during the thirteenth century, which in general was favorable to the renascence of Church Slavonic culture among the Southern Slavs. In the Czech state this use was abolished toward the beginning of the twelfth century, but its tradition contributed to the rise of a Bohemian vernacular literature in the late thirteenth. In the fourteenth and fifteenth centuries, besides highly developed

7

belles-lettres, even Czech science and philosophy turned to the national language and adapted it to the Latin cultural pattern. Rich terminological dictionaries were elaborated; attempts at holding church services in the mother tongue were made, and under the Hussites they became a contagious precedent for the European Reformation. After a weakening of its foremost position in the late seventeenth and eighteenth centuries, literary Czech resurged with the nineteenth century, exploiting the old heritage, borrowing from other Slavic languages (especially from Polish), and quickly adapted to modern cultural needs. The Polish literary language, which especially in the fourteenth and fifteenth centuries had been modeled on Czech (the language of the Polish world of fashion until the sixteenth century), reached a world status, first in sixteenth-century poetry and then in Romanticism. In the sixteenth century the Reformation inspired religious texts for the Slovenian, Sorbian, and Kashubian people in their mother tongues. The propaganda of the Counter Reformation, endeavoring to penetrate to the populace, and later the democratic tendencies of the nineteenth century reinforced these vernacular literatures. Particularly modern Slovenian scholarship and literature and their means of expression attained a high level. In both of the smallest of the Slavic speech communities striving for the literary use of their vernacular, the champion writers were American emigrants —the Kashub H. Derdowski (1852–1902) and the Low Sorbian poet Mato Kósyk (1853–1940).

During the whole of the Middle Ages the written literature of Greek Orthodox Slavs was prevailingly ecclesiastic and used Church Slavonic; lay documents and juridical texts, however, were written in the local vernacular. Secular literary works, such as fiction, chronicles, profane itineraries, etc., oscillated between Church Slavonic and the vernacular. Even though the last three centuries have strongly secularized Russian culture and strengthened the vernacular (Middle Russian) stratum in the literary tongue, its traditional hybrid structure, which differentiates Church Slavonic and folk components semantically and stylistically and distributes them in various ways, has remained the pivotal principle of modern Standard Russian and is still the main source of its unusual richness. The political conditions of the Moscovite period created two distinct variants of the Eastern Slavic literary language: the Great-Russian pattern on the one hand, and the Southwestern on the other, which, besides a Moscow influence, exhibited a Ukrainian and locally a Byelo-Russian ingredient and which, moreover, was somewhat occidentalized through the Czech and Polish intermediary. To overcome this split, the patriarch Nikon, after the incorporation of the Ukraine into the Moscow Tsardom in the middle of the seventeenth century, initiated a radical revision of the Russian liturgic and literary language along Kievan lines. This reform contributed to the gradual Westernization of Standard Russian which in different ways during the seventeenth century imported a large number of Polish and Czech words, and then under Peter, directly followed Germanic and later on Romance models.

After a rich development in the thirteenth and fourteenth centuries, Church Slavonic literature waned in Bulgaria and suffered a decline in Serbia with the Turkish invasion, diffusing at the same time a Balkan influence on both Southern and Northern Russia's literary language and giving birth as well to a new, RUMANIAN recension of Church Slavonic which served as the literary and liturgic language of Rumanians from the late fourteenth to the eighteenth century. Toward the sixteenth century, even in the Ottoman court and administration, Balkan Slavic speech came into use. On the other hand, the spiritual life and literary language of Serbia in the seventeenth century underwent a still greater Russian influence, and in the eighteenth century the native recension of Church Slavonic was replaced by the Russian pattern. In that part of the Serbocroatian world which adhered to Western Christianity there appeared, partly under the influence of the Reformation, partly after the model of the Italian Renaissance, regional attempts at raising the vernacular to a literary language with a Church Slavonic tinge. The most fertile of these were the Dalmatian schools of poetry—the western one flourished in the sixteenth century, and that of Dubrovnik (Ragusa) in the sixteenth and seventeenth. But the modern standard language, unifying both Serbs and Croats, which developed during the first half of the nineteenth century, was only sporadically linked with earlier attempts: it raised to literary usage a folk dialect of Herzegovina and emphatically rejected Church Slavonic or Russian ingredients and the influence of any older literary heritage. A similar populist tendency characterized the rise at the same period of modern literary Ukrainian which was first used in the burlesques of the very late eighteenth century, and in its further development oscillated between the Western (Polish-influenced) and the Eastern (Russian-influenced) variants. Both Standard Byelo-Russian and Macedonian modestly entered into literature in the nineteenth century and acquired civil rights—the former after the First, the latter after the Second World War. On the other hand, modern Standard Bulgarian, likewise formed during the nineteenth century after some isolated earlier attempts, strongly and consistently continued to borrow from Russian and particularly from its Church Slavonic stock. Toward the middle of the same century, the Slovaks, who had used literary Czech (somewhat adapted to their own habits), inaugurated their own literary language based on the Central Slovak dialect but patterned after standard Czech.

Church Slavonic perseveres as a liturgic language in several slightly distinct variants: Nikon's recension is used by Greek Orthodox Slavs (and—with somewhat stronger orientation toward the old Kievan tradition—by the Greek Catholics); the pre-Nikon, Great-Russian recension is followed by the Old Believers; the Croatian Roman Catholics, in so far as they use Church Slavonic, maintain their own recension, although since the seventeenth century they have incorporated a considerable Kievan strain.

In the Slavic standard languages, besides Greek influence, prevailing in the area of the Eastern Church, and Latin, predominant in that of the Western, there can be noted a strong Turkic lexical layer in Eastern Slavic and in the majority of Southern Slavic languages, and a German stamp on the vocabulary and phraseology of Slovenian and of Western Slavic languages and on the technical terminology of modern Russian. To some degree all the main Slavic literary languages in their recent phase bear French imprints. Neighboring languages have undergone an appreciable Slavic influence, principally in their vocabulary. This is particularly so for the Baltic languages, Albanian, Greek, Rumanian, Yiddish (in the syntax of the latter two, as well), for Gipsy in Slavic environment, for most of the Uralic, Altaic, and Paleosiberian languages, and for Aleut and Alaska Eskimo.

Systems of Writing. In order to symbolize the sovereignity of the Slavic language, St. Cyril invented a quite distinct alphabet, adapting and modifying certain Greek, Samaritan, perhaps Coptic, and other Oriental letters. This alphabet, called GLAGOLITIC, was used in Great Moravia, and then in Bohemia and Croatia, Macedonia, and partly in Bulgaria. In the latter country it met strong competition from the so-called CYRILLIC alphabet which had been created there at the beginning of the tenth century to bring Slavic writing closer to the Greek—both Slavic alphabets occur in the fragmentary inscriptions of Preslava from the early tenth century. Cyrillic won out in all of the Greek Orthodox Slavic countries and is still used there in the Church, while for lay purposes it was refashioned under Peter the Great and the shape of the letters brought closer to the Latin: this modification spread from Russia to all Slavs of the Eastern rite. Since the twelfth century the Glagolitic alphabet has been limited to Croatia, except for isolated attempts of single Czech and Polish monasteries to borrow this Croatian habit in the fourteenth–fifteenth centuries. With the sixteenth century it began to disappear from secular Croatian writings and the area of its Church usage has become more and more limited, but after the Second World War spadework has been undertaken among Slavic Benedictines for a new extension of the Slavonic liturgy. With these exceptions all the Catholic Slavs now use the Latin alphabet. The fourteenth century Czech system of expressing those phonemes which have no graphic symbols in the Latin alphabet by various digraphs is still the basis for Polish spelling, whereas the Czechs have introduced the diacritic system, first tried by Jan Hus under the influence of the Glagolitic alphabet. This kind of spelling is now general for all Slavs of Western denominations with the exception of Poles and Kashubs.

SAMPLES

SINCE the Gospel has been universally translated, a sample may be selected from it in the various Slavic languages. We choose the colloquial sentence from St. Luke 10.35 (using and completing Nahtigal's quotations in his Slovanski jeziki and applying the American scholarly transliteration for the non-Latin alphabets): 'Take care of him: and whatsoever thou spendest more, when I come again, I will repay thee.'

Old Church Slavonic (Bulgarian recension): prileži emь. i eže ašte priiždiveši. azъ egda vъzvraštǫ sę vъzdamь ti.

Modern Greek Orthodox (Cyrillic) Church Slavonic: prileži jemu: i, ježe ašče priiždiveši, az, jegda vozvraščusja, vozdam ti.

Modern Roman Catholic (Glagolitic) Church Slavonic: Prileži jemu, i ježe ašće priiždiveši, az jegda vazvraću se, vzdam ti.

Russian: pozabot'sja o nëm; i esli izderžiš' čto bolee, ja vernuvšis' (or kogda vozvraščus'), otdam tebe.

Ukrainian: Dohljadaj joho, i ščo nad se vydasy, ja, vernuvšys', oddam tobi.

Byelo-Russian: dahljadaj jaho i, kali vydaš što balej, ja, vjarnuwšysja, addam tabe.

Polish: Miej o nim staranie, a cokolwiek nad to wynałożysz, ja, gdy się wrócę, oddam ci.

Kashubian: Mnjej ŭo njim stôranji, a cokolwjek nad to wëdôsz, jô, ciej sę wrócę, ŭoddôm cé.

Low Sorbian: Zastaraj jogo, a cožkuli wěcej nałožyš, zapłaśim tebje, gaž se vrośim.

High Sorbian: Zastaraj jeho, a štožkuli wjacy wułožiš, zapłaću tebi, hdyž so wróću.

Czech: Měj o něj péči, a cožkoli nad to vynaložíš, já když se vrátím, zaplatím tobě.

Slovak: Maj na neho starost', a čo by si nad to viacej vynaložil, ja ti, ked' zase prijdem, zaplatím.

Slovenian: Poskrbi zanj, in kar boš več potrošil, ti jaz nazaj gredé povrnem.

Serbocroatian: Gledaj ga, i što više potrošiš ja ću ti platiti kad se vratim.

Macedonian: Zagriži se za nego, i što ke izarčiš ke ti platam koga ke se vratam.

Bulgarian: Pogriži se za nego; i kakvoto poveče iždiviš, na vrъštane az šte ti zaplatja.

COMPARATIVE PHONOLOGY

THE CHARACTERISTIC tendencies of Slavic evolution before the dissolution of unity are: (A) the complete abolition of aspiration (a loss common to all those Indo-European branches which did not set up a new h phoneme), and the persevering clear-cut opposition of voicing and voicelessness; (B) the consistent opposition of front and back vowels and accordingly that of 'soft' and 'hard' syllables, achieved by all kinds of mutual adaptation between vowels and adjacent consonants; (C) the recasting of prothetic semivowels (at the beginning of the word certain vowels require either the presence or the avoidance of an initial v, while other vowels that of an initial j); (D) the change of the short u and i into reduced vowels ('jers,' according to their Church Slavonic spelling name), the back ъ and the front ь; (E) the gradual elimination of closed syllables: loss of final consonants, simplification of consonantal clusters, reshaping of all diphthongs ending in u and i ($ou > \bar{u}$; $ei > \bar{i}$; $oi > \bar{e}$, but in final position oi is represented either by $\bar{e}$ or by $\bar{i}$, going back to a difference in quantity), suppression of tautosyllabic groups 'vowel (dialectally only the non-reduced one) plus liquid or nasal': in initial position the group $\check{o}r* > ra$; $\check{o}r > ra$ only in the South Slavic area and Central Slovak, and $> ro$ elsewhere; between consonants the groups $\check{o}r$ and $\check{o}r$ (1) changed into ra in the South Slavic and Czechoslovak area (with a parallel mutation of $ъr$ into $r̥$), (2) dissolved into a disyllabic sequence—Polish-Sorbian $tъrot$ (with a metathesis) and East Slavic $torot$ (without a metathesis), (3) merged with $ъr$ in North-Lekhitic; in those Slavic dialects where the groups on, en preserved the nasal, they were changed into $ъn$, $ьn$; (F) substitution of qualitative for old quantitative distinctions and development of new quantitative vocalic oppositions;

---

* r in these formulas stands for any liquid, o for any open non-reduced vowel, $ъ$ for any reduced vowel, t for any consonant.

13

(G) a prosodic pattern based on opposition of rising and falling pitch both in long and short syllables, with word-accent appended to the rising pitch and, in its absence, to the initial syllable (while the Balto-Slavic prosodic pattern had tolerated the word-accent on the second mora of any long syllable and on the initial or final mora of the word).

During the second half of the first millennium A.D., the diffusion of innovations within the vast Slavic area became slower, and in particular regional divergences in their temporal order gave rise to certain dialectal features. Differently treated are: prothetic semivowels; vowels plus tautosyllabic liquids and nasals; *ě* (called *jat'*, the reflex of *ē* and *oi*); on the one hand the clusters *tj* and *dj*, and on the other, the fricative *x* when preceded by certain front vowels and followed by certain back vowels ('progressive palatalization') and furthermore, *x* before the reflexes of *oi* ('second regressive palatalization'): either only this *x* or only *tj*, *dj* become hissing sounds; *j* after non-initial labials; *t*, *d* before *l* and nasals; velars before the reflex of *woi*; front vowels before dentals followed by back vowels; the prosodic variety of the accented syllables (long and short, both either falling or rising) which underwent diverse regional modifications and limitations.

Some of the local innovations within the final Protoslavic period serve (1) to distinguish Eastern Slavic (*tort* > *torot*, ъ in *tъrt* had the same treatment as the strong ъ before obstruents, *dj* > *ž*, *bdm* > *m*, initial *j* disappeared before *u* and under certain conditions before *e* becoming *o*), and (2) to divide it into two dialects— Northern (the affricates *č* and *c* coalesced) and Southern (*g* became fricative): North Russian derives from the former, and the other Eastern Slavic speech-varieties from the latter dialect. The difference between Russian and Ukrainian will come later, in the twelfth–thirteenth century, when the tendency to use a common phonemic pattern still persists, but the etymological distribution of these phonemes is already somewhat different (e.g., both Russian and Ukrainian at that time developed the same diphthong *uo*, with the same prothetic *v* in initial position, but in Ukrainian, *uo* originates from *o* before a dropped 'jer,' and in Russian, from *o* under a rising accent). The formation of Byelo-Russian as a

14

whole will not start until the fifteenth century with its strengthening Polish influence.

Some dialectal innovations within the final Protoslavic period are common to the whole Western Slavic group (*tj*, *dj* changed to hissing sounds; all the palatalizations of *x* gave *š*). Except the change of the final group *jōns* into *en* in the Slavic South, and *ě* in the West and North, there are no common, exclusively Southern Slavic innovations: some changes link Southern with Eastern Slavic (velars undergoing the second palatalization were changed into hissing sounds; after labials *j* gave a palatal *l*; *d*, *t* were lost before *l* and *n* except in some marginal Slovenian dialects and in Pskov-Russian); some other changes link the Southern group with Czechoslovak or at least with its eastern variant now represented by Central Slovak. Certain mutations were undergone by the whole central Slavic area (e.g., change of *g* into a fricative, attested in Czech, Slovak, High Sorbian, Ukrainian, Byelo-Russian, South Great-Russian, and part of Slovenian). A wider spread of central isoglosses as opposed to a marginal pattern is the oscillation of 'ě' between *e* and *i* and the connected change of the tautosyllabic groups *on*, *en* to the back and front vowels of the lowest timbre (*u* and mostly *ę*) everywhere except in the Lekhitic, Bulgaro-Macedonian, and in a part of the Slovenian area: here 'ě' oscillates between *e* and *a*, while *on*, *en* became ъn, ьn; still preserved is the nasal component in the Lekhitic languages and in some border dialects of Slovenian and Macedonian.

The loss of the 'jers,' a feature which expanded slowly in the tenth–twelfth centuries from the Southwest to the Northeast of the Slavic world, was the last common Slavic mutation. Throughout the whole of the Slavic area the 'jers' were lost with one essential limitation: of the two 'jers' in the neighboring syllables, the last (called 'weak') was dropped but the preceding (called 'strong') changed into an unreduced vowel. The loss of the 'jers' destroyed the uniformity of the Slavic syllable—its openness and the harmony of its constituents—and therewith forced the prosodic reshaping of the Slavic languages. (1) *A*. Serbocroatian and Slovenian, and *B*. North Kashubian maintained or partly restored both distinctive features of Protoslavic word-prosody—pitch and quantity: type *A* maintaining and *B* eliminating the quantitative opposition under accent. (2) Having abolished the rising pitch, Czech and Slovak, except for some transitional dialects, automatically fixed the accent on the initial syllable and maintained free quantity. On the contrary, the Eastern Slavic area and Bulgarian, with the adjacent Macedonian strip, abolished quantity in favor of free stress (this evolution is bound up with avoidance of vocalic contraction, whereas the maintenance of quantity implies new long vowels due to contraction). The intermediary zone between the languages with free quantity and those with free stress now presents neither quantity nor free stress—the latter is stabilized on the penult in Polish, Eastern Slovak, and Rusnak, on the first syllable in Sorbian and Southern Kashubian, on the antepenult in Western Macedonian. Thus we distinguish languages (3) without free stress and quantity and (4) with free stress.

The latter two types have a higher number of consonantal phonemes and clusters, the former two, especially the first one, a greater number of vocalic phonemes. The liquids assume a syllabic function only in the phonemic patterns of types 1A and 2; Czech excepted, they participate in the quantitative opposition. Type 4 tends to reduce the number of vocalic phonemes in un-stressed position (e.g., to four in North Russian, to three—*u, a, i*—in South Russian and Byelo-Russian); type 1A reduces the pho-nemic inventory of velar consonants (mostly losing *x*, and in some Slovenian dialects even *k* and *g*). Only types 3 and 4 tolerate double consonants. Before losing the weak 'jers,' all Slavic dialects, except 1A, maintained the difference between ъ and ь and between the preceding consonants—palatalized before front vowel but not before back vowel. With the loss of the weak 'jers' this con-sonantal difference became phonemic, but in various ways was then gradually eliminated by 1B and 2, whereas the whole area 4 and most of the intermediary area 3 preserved or even strengthened this opposition. Except Slovenian and Kashubian, the languages which either did not develop or lost palatalization (softness) as a distinctive feature, acquired in different ways a fourth, palatal series of stops besides the labials, dentals, and velars (particularly so in Serbocroatian, Czech, and Slovak). Except for Slovenian,

16

Serbocroatian, and some Bulgarian dialects where ъ and ь in strong position coalesced into ə or a, the strong ь in all languages became e, while ъ changed to o in the whole Eastern Slavic area, in Macedonia, partly also in High Sorbian and Central Slovak; everywhere else it changed to a corresponding unrounded vowel which later in 2 and 3 (but never in 4) coalesced with e. The vocalic phonemes of 4 are determined by the opposition of rounded and unrounded; and to the South moreover, the unrounded series splits into front and back: both for the higher and for the lower vowels the Ukrainian and the Bulgarian phonemic pattern distinguishes (a) unrounded front, (b) unrounded back, (c) rounded (back). The change of long vowels into decrescent diphthongs occurs only in the Western borderland of the Slavic world—in Czech, Polabian, and Kashubian.

In various regions of the Slavic world—in some Russian, Polish, Sorbian, and Serbocroatian dialects—the hushing and the corresponding hissing affricates, or generally sibilants, coalesced. A rare phoneme, the sibilant vibrant r, formerly common to the majority of the Western Slavic languages, is maintained in Czech and Kashubian.

COMPARATIVE GRAMMAR

THE AUTONOMY of the word and the markedness of word boundaries are preserved both in Protoslavic and in the modern Slavic languages; and there is a clear-cut difference between the treatment of affixes on one hand, and proclitic conjunctions or enclitic particles on the other. The root plus derivational and inflectional suffixes forms a simple word. A root preceded by another root or by a prefix produces a complex word. Prepositions are phonemically treated as prefixes. Derivational suffixes remain an extremely productive means for neology in Slavic languages. Prefixes play only a derivational role but prefixation as such has an important part in the building of Slavic verbal aspects. Alternations of phonemes are relevant auxiliary means in Slavic inflection; pivotal are prosodic alternations both in Protoslavic and in those Slavic languages which maintain in their word structure such

17

distinctive features as pitch, quantity, or place of accent; as a result of the loss of the 'jers' alternations of vowel and zero as well as zero desinences occupy a great place in all Slavic languages. Autonomous alternations of different vowels in the root are in part the residue of Indo-European or Protoslavic processes, and in part essential innovations of separate Slavic languages, e.g., Ukrainian, Polish, Czech. In desinences vocalic alternations conditioned by the stem-end (a characteristic feature of late Protoslavic), remain, in spite of all analogic changes, a pertinent factor in the morphologic structure of modern Slavic languages. Due to various palatalization processes, the alternations of the last stem-consonant are partly inherited from Protoslavic, partly developed in the separate Slavic languages. There is still a pronounced tendency (particularly striking in Russian) to differentiate the alternations used in declension and those used in conjugation.

Protoslavic preserved the Indo-European system of cases (Nom., Acc., Instr., Dat., Gen., Loc.), losing only the ablative which merged with the genitive—the latter took over the ablative desinence for o-stems. The use of m in the Instr. and Dat. desinences links Slavic with the Baltic and Germanic area. The nominal declension exhibits a strong influence from the pronominal, an interaction of different paradigms, and a tendency to identify paradigms with genders. The impulse to unify the declension continues in separate Slavic languages. All of them tend to eliminate the prepositionless use of the Loc. and of the Dat. of destination. The substitution of the possessive Gen. for the original possessive adjective is widespread. Western and Eastern Slavic languages developed a predicative Instr. Bulgarian and Macedonian, for the most part, have lost declension (as well as the suffixal comparative forms of the adjectives) and developed instead a postpositive article. Distinction of single cases, weakened both formally and functionally in Sorbian, Czech, Slovenian, and Serbocroatian, is firmly held in the other Slavic languages and even enriched by two new cases (Gen. 2 and Loc. 2) in Russian, and the general meanings of the cases remain here distinctly delimited (e.g., the persistence of the Gen. of negation perfectly fits the general meaning of the genitive as a purely restrictive case). The vocative form is preserved in all Slavic languages except Russian and Slovenian.

A sharp distinction between the singular and the plural unvaryingly goes through the whole Slavic inflection, whereas the dual, still vital in the Slavic medieval world, died out but for Slovenian, Sorbian, and Slovincian. Residues of the old nominal dual serve to denote nouns after numerals from 'two' to 'four' in Russian and Serbocroatian, and after all numerals in Bulgarian which, along with declension, lost the clear-cut Slavic difference between the substantivized numerals from 'five' and the lower numerals consistently adjectivized. Slavic substantives and adjectives still strikingly distinguish masculine, feminine, and neuter in the singular; in the plural, however, these distinctions are lost by Russian and Bulgarian and tend to weaken as well elsewhere. The difference between the animate and inanimate started for the Acc. Sg. M. in late Protoslavic and became generalized for some other cases in Western Slavic languages, and for the Acc. Pl. in Russian. Bulgarian, Western Slavic languages (particularly Polish and Sorbian), and Ukrainian tend to promote a new, personal gender.

For the adjectives Protoslavic developed a new, definite form which distinguishes more clearly their declension from that of the substantives. In Serbocroatian and Slovenian the difference between the definite and indefinite forms is more or less preserved and marked by prosodic alternations; Bulgarian and Macedonian have reduced the use of the definite form, whereas Byelo-Russian, Ukrainian, and Western Slavic languages tend to eliminate the indefinite doublet; Russian has changed it into a purely predicative, indeclinable form.

The Protoslavic verb had been more essentially reshaped than the noun. Only the forms of the present tense continue closely an Indo-European prototype; the forms of the aorist are perceptibly refashioned, while the forms of the Slavic imperfect have nothing in common with the Indo-European stock. Neither the form nor the function of the Indo-European perfect find correspondence in the Slavic. Besides two sets of simple forms—the sequential past (the so-called 'aorist') and the synchronic past (the so-called 'imperfect'), Slavic created new, compound pasts: the retrospective

19

past (inadequately called the 'perfect'), and three pluperfects corresponding to the aorist, the imperfect, and the perfect. Protoslavic abolished the Indo-European subjunctive and innovated a compound conditional. The Indo-European optative was re-formed into an imperative, whereas the old imperative disappeared completely. The middle voice became obsolete and its functions were partly assumed by the Slavic (and Baltic) construction with the enclitic Acc. of the reflexive pronoun which had been generalized for all persons; besides, a periphrastic passive was developing with verbal adjectives changed into participles. The nominal forms of the verb, the infinitive and supine, are due to a convergent development in the Slavic and some other Indo-European dialects. Partly paralleled by the Baltic, Protoslavic developed a system of coupled verbs of perfective (denoting the completion of a process) and imperfective (without such denotation) aspect; of the imperfective verbs a few couples denote the opposition of determined (characterizing the process as an uninterrupted whole) and undetermined aspect. The future was usually expressed by either the present of perfective verbs or different periphrastic constructions with imperfective verbs. Various types of impersonal constructions were developed with a zero-subject and a verb in 3rd pers. Sg. or Pl. as predicate. Conjugation drew upon two stems, one full and another truncated, chiefly regular in their alternation (depending on the vocalic or consonantal onset of the desinence)—a feature which has persisted for the most part to the present time.

This rich set of verbal forms (in Old Church Slavonic an imperfective verb had up to 236 forms, without counting the compound ones) persisted fundamentally through the Middle Ages. Later, most of the Slavic languages generalized the original 'perfect' as the only past; the imperfect and the aorist have been kept only in Sorbian on the one hand, and in Bulgarian, Macedonian, and Serbocroatian on the other. These same Southern Slavic languages stabilized the use of the verb *xъtěti* 'want' for the compound future and generalized this construction for the perfective verbs as well, somewhat dampening (as Sorbian also does) the opposition of the aspects. Bulgarian and Macedonian have developed the richest pattern of finite forms with a consistent opposition of direct and indirect narration. Fundamentally, the Protoslavic pattern of aspects, voices, and moods is preserved in all Slavic languages. The imperative becomes (especially in Russian and Ukrainian) a bare stem, agglutinating autonomous suffixes phonemically treated as particles. The supine remained only in Low Sorbian and Slovenian. The infinitive is lost in Bulgarian and Macedonian. Participles tended at an early date to do away with declension and to become gerunds—in the Eastern and partly also in the Western Slavic area they even lost gender and number.

Enclitics traditionally followed the first accented word, but in languages with free stress the inflected enclitics were attracted by the governing word and then completely eliminated in the whole Eastern Slavic area, except for Western Ukrainian dialects: in the reflexive verbs the pronoun became an inseparable suffix; the other pronominal enclitic forms, richly developed in Protoslavic, were lost; the auxiliary verb as used in the 3rd pers. Sg. Neutr. of the compound forms was generalized (in the conditional *by* and in the pluperfect *bylo* became mere particles); in the 'perfect' the pres. 3rd pers. zero-form of the auxiliary verb *byti* 'be,' when used for all persons, changed the 'perfect' into a simple form. Subsequently the present of *byti* was likewise omitted in its other functions and the use of the correlative verb *iměti* 'have' essentially reduced; the abolishment of the copula favored asyndeton; finally, in personal constructions the use of pronouns, which was pleonastic for the Slavic pattern, became normal and their omission, which was normal for the Slavic pattern, became elliptic.

Word order underwent some alterations in the separate development of the Slavic languages. Particularly the verb tends to a medial position in the sentence and the place of attributes depends on regional changes in the system of definite and indefinite adjectives. Generally, word order is still based on the same principles as in Protoslavic: there is one basic pattern and a set of usual deviations each of which possesses a distinct semantic or stylistic value. In the spoken Slavic languages hypotaxis is weakly developed and less used than parataxis. The evolution of Slavic languages shows an extreme instability of conjunctions and relative pronouns.

21

SELECTED BIBLIOGRAPHY*

COMPARATIVE SLAVIC PHILOLOGY

Contemporary Slavic languages and their sound pattern

R. Trautmann, Die slavischen Völker und Sprachen, Göttingen, 1947. O. Broch, Slavische Phonetik, Heidelberg, 1911. H. Rubenstein, A comparative study of morphophonemic alternations in standard Serbo-Croatian, Czech and Russian, Ann Arbor, 1950.

Comparative historical surveys

R. Nahtigal, Slovanski jeziki, 2d ed., Ljubljana, 1952. V. Vondrák, Vergleichende slavische Grammatik, vols. 1–2, 2d ed., Göttingen, 1924–29. A. Seliščev, Slavjanskoe jazykoznanie, vol. 1, Moscow, 1941.

Primitive Slavic and its dissolution

A. Meillet, Le slave commun, 2d ed., Paris, 1934. J. Mikkola, Urslavische Grammatik, vols. 1–3, Heidelberg, 1913–50. J. Kořínek, Od indoeuropského prajazyka k praslovančine, Bratislava, 1948. N. van Wijk, Les langues slaves: de l'unité à la pluralité, Paris, 1937.

Phonology

R. Jakobson, Remarques sur l'évolution phonologique du russe comparée à celle des autres langues slaves, Prague, 1929. J. Kuryłowicz, L'accentuation des langues indo-européennes, Chapter III: Le balto–slave, Cracow, 1952. D. Bubrich, "Du système d'accentuation en slave commun," *Revue des études slaves*, vol. 6, 1926.

Morphology

O. Hujer, Slovanská deklinace jmenná, Prague, 1910. C. Stang, Das slavische und baltische Verbum, Oslo, 1942. B. Havránek, Genera verbi v slovanských jazycích, vols. 1–2, Prague, 1928–37. C. G. Regnéll, Über den Ursprung des slavischen Verbalaspektes, Lund, 1944.

* The author acknowledges with thanks the help of Professors H. Lunt, G. Shevelov, and W. Weintraub.

Syntax

F. Miklosich, Vergleichende Grammatik der slavischen Sprachen, vol. 4: Syntax, reprint, Heidelberg, 1926.

Dictionaries

R. Trautmann, Baltisch-slawisches Wörterbuch, Göttingen, 1923. E. Berneker, Slavisches etymologisches Wörterbuch, vol. 1, Heidelberg, 1913. F. Miklošič, Kratkij slovar' šesti slavjanskix jazykov, Vienna, 1885.

Practical manual in English

R. G. A. De Bray, Guide to the Slavonic languages, London, 1951.

CHURCH SLAVONIC

Descriptive grammars of Old Church Slavonic

H. Lunt, Old Church Slavonic Grammar, The Hague, 1955. N. Trubetzkoy, Altkirchenslavische Grammatik, Vienna, 1954. P. Diels, Altkirchenslavische Grammatik, vols. 1–2, Heidelberg, 1932–34. A. Vaillant, Manuel du vieux slave, vols. 1–2, Paris, 1948. M. Halle, "The Old Church Slavonic Conjugation," *Word*, vol. 7, 1951.

History of Old Church Slavonic

N. van Wijk, Geschichte der altkirchenslavischen Sprache, Berlin, 1931. J. Jagić, Entstehungsgeschichte der kirchenslavischen Sprache, 2d ed., Berlin, 1913.

A non-Slavic recension of Church Slavonic

D. Bogdan, Caracterul limbii textelor slavo-române, Bucharest, 1946.

Dictionaries and lexical studies

F. Miklosich, Lexicon palaeoslovenico-graeco-latinum, Vienna, 1862–65. G. D'jačenko, Polnyj cerkovno-slavjanskij slovar', Moscow, 1899. L. Sadnik and R. Aitzetmüller, Handwörterbuch zu den altkirchenslavischen Texten, Heidelberg, 1955. A. Meillet, Etudes sur l'étymologie et vocabulaire du vieux slave vols. 1–2, Paris, 1902–3.

23

Contemporary Russian

L. Bulaxovskij, Kurs russkogo literaturnogo jazyka, 5th ed., Kiev, 1952. R. Košutić, Gramatika ruskog jezika, vol. 1, Petrograd, 1919; vol. 2, Belgrade, 1914. R. Avanesov and I. Sidorov, Očerk grammatiki russkogo literaturnogo jazyka, Moscow, 1945. N. Durnovo, Povtoritel'nyj kurs grammatiki russkogo jazyka, vols. 1–2, Moscow, 1924–29. Akademija Nauk SSSR, Grammatika russkogo jazyka, vols. 1-2, Moscow, 1953-54.

Sound pattern of contemporary Russian

S. C. Boyanus, Russian pronunciation together with a Russian phonetic reader, London, 1954. R. Avanesov, Russkoe literaturnoe proiznošenie, Moscow, 1950. G. Vinokur, Russkoe sceničeskoe proiznošenie, Moscow, 1948.

Morphology

V. Vinogradov, Russkij jazyk (grammatičeskoe učenie o slove), Moscow, 1947. R. Jakobson, "Beitrag zur allgemeinen Kasuslehre," *Travaux du Cercle Linguistique de Prague*, vol. 6, 1936. S. Obnorskij, Imennoe sklonenie v sovremennom russkom jazyke, vols. 1–2, Leningrad, 1927–31. S. Karcevski, Système du verbe russe, Prague, 1927. R. Jakobson, "Russian conjugation," *Word*, vol. 4, 1948. S. Obnorskij, Očerki po morfologii russkogo glagola, Moscow, 1953.

Syntax

A. Šaxmatov, Sintaksis russkogo jazyka, 2d ed., Leningrad, 1941. A. Peškovskij, Russkij sintaksis v naučnom otnošenii, 4th ed., Moscow, 1934. M. Peterson, Očerk sintaksisa russkogo jazyka, Moscow, 1923.

Dialectology

W. Matthews, "Modern Russian dialects," *Transactions of the Philological Society*, 1950. R. Avanesov, Očerki russkoj dialektologii, Moscow, 1949. P. Kuznecov, Russkaja dialektologija, Moscow, 1951. A. Šapiro, Očerki po sintaksisu russkix narodnyx govorov, Moscow, 1953.

History of East Slavic languages, especially Russian

G. Vinokur, Russkij jazyk, Moscow, 1945 (French translation, Paris, 1947; German, Leipzig, 1949). N. Durnovo, Vvedenie v istoriju russkogo jazyka, Brno, 1927. N. Durnovo, Očerk istorii russkogo jazyka, Moscow, 1924. L. Jakubinskij, Istorija drevnerusskogo jazyka, Moscow, 1953. P. Černyx, Istoričeskaja grammatika russkogo jazyka, Moscow, 1952. A. Šaxmatov, Kurs istorii russkogo jazyka, vols. 1–3, St. Petersburg, 1911–16.

Historical morphology

P. Kuznecov, Istoričeskaja grammatika russkogo jazyka: morfologija, Moscow, 1953. B. Unbegaun, La langue russe au 16ᵉ siècle: la flexion des noms, Paris, 1935. S. Nikiforov, Glagol, ego kategorii i formy v russkoj pis'mennosti vtoroj poloviny XVI veka, Moscow, 1952.

History of literary Russian

S. Nikiforov, Istorija russkogo literaturnogo jazyka, Moscow, 1947. N. Trubetzkoy, Common Slavic element in Russian culture, New York, 1949. L. Bulaxovskij, Istoričeskij kommentarij k literaturnomu russkomu jazyku, 3d ed., Kiev, 1950. V. Vinogradov, Očerki po istorii russkogo literaturnogo jazyka 17–19 vv.; reprint of the 2d ed., Leiden, 1950.

Dictionaries of contemporary Russian

D. Dal', Tolkovyj slovar' živogo velikorusskogo jazyka, vols. 1–4; reprint of the 4th ed., Tokyo, 1934. D. Ušakov, Tolkovyj slovar' russkogo jazyka, vols 1–4; reprint, Ann Arbor, 1948. Akademija Nauk SSSR, Slovar' sovremennogo russkogo jazyka, 1st 3 vols., Leningrad, 1950–54.

Dictionaries of Old Russian

I. Sreznevskij, Materialy dlja slovarja drevnerusskogo jazyka po pis'mennym pamjatnikam, vols. 1–3, St. Petersburg, 1893–1912. G. Kočin, Materialy dlja terminologičeskogo slovarja drevnej Rossii, Leningrad, 1937.

Etymological dictionaries

A. Preobraženskij, Ètimologičeskij slovar' russkogo jazyka; reprint, New York, 1951. M. Vasmer, Russisches etymologisches Wörterbuch, Heidelberg, from 1951.

Guides and practical manuals in English

A. Smirnickij, Russko-anglijskij slovar', Moscow, 1949. V. K. Müller, Anglo-russkij slovar', 3d ed., Moscow, 1950. S. Boyanus and N. Jopson, Spoken Russian, a practical course, London, 1939. B. Unbegaun and J. Simmons, A bibliographical guide to the Russian language, Oxford, 1953.

UKRAINIAN

Contemporary Ukrainian

J. Šerex, Narys sučasnoji ukrajins'koji literaturnoji movy, Munich, 1951. L. Bulaxovs'kyj (ed.), Kurs sučasnoji ukrajins'-koji literaturnoji movy, vols. 1–2, Kiev, 1951. O. Synjavs'kyj, Normy ukrajins'koji literaturnoji movy, 2d ed., Lwow, 1941. V. Simovyč, Gramatyka ukrajins'koji movy, 2d ed., Kiev-Leipzig, 1919.

Sound pattern

J. Ziłyński, Opis fonetyczny języka ukraińskiego, Cracow, 1932.

Syntax

S. Smerečyns'kyj, Narysy z ukrajins'koji syntaksy, Kharkov, 1932.

Dialectology

V. Hancov, Dijalektolohična klasyfikacija ukrajins'kyx hovoriv, Kiev, 1923. I. Zilyns'kyj, Karta ukrajins'kyx hovoriv, Warsaw, 1933.

History of Ukrainian

E. Tymčenko, Kurs istoriji ukrajins'kogo jazyka, Kiev, 1927. P. Buzuk, Narys istoriji ukrajins'koji movy, Kiev, 1927. A. Šaxmatov and A. Kryms'kyj, Narysy z istoriji ukrajins'koji movy ta xrestomatija, Kiev, 1924. S. Kul'bakin, Ukrainskij jazyk, Kharkov, 1919.

History of literary Ukrainian

Mitropolit Ilarion, Istorija ukrajins'koji literaturnoji movy, Winnipeg, 1949.

Dictionaries of contemporary Ukrainian

B. Hrinčenko, Slovar' ukrajins'koji movy, 2d ed., Berlin, 1924. I. Kyryčenko, T. Zajceva and M. Ќyl's'kyj, Ukrajins'ko-rosijs'kyj slovnyk I, Kiev, 1953. M. Kalinovič, Russko-ukrainskij slovar', Moscow, 1948.

Historical dictionary

J. Tymčenko, Istoryčnyj slovnyk ukrajins'koho jazyka, vol. 1, Kharkov, 1930.

Guides and practical manuals in English

M. Podvez'ko, Ukrajins'ko-anglijs'kyj slovnyk, Kiev, 1952. G. Luckyj and J. B. Rudnyckyj, A modern Ukrainian grammar, Minneapolis, 1949.

BYELO-RUSSIAN

Contemporary Byelo-Russian

T. Lomtev, Belorusskij jazyk, Moscow, 1951. J. Lësik, Hramatyka belaruskae movy, 3 vols., Minsk, 1925–27.

Sound pattern and morphology

K. Hurski, T. Lomcew, H. Škljar, and S. Roxkind, Kurs sučasnaj belaruskaj movy: Fonetyka, morfolohija, leksyka, Minsk, 1940.

Syntax

J. Kolas,. K. Hurski, and H. Škljar, Sintaksis belaruskaj movy, Minsk, 1939.

Dialectology

P. Buzuk, Sproba linhvystičnoji heohrafiji Belarusi, Minsk, 1928.

History

P. Rastorguev, "Belorusskaja reč' v ee sovremennom i prošlom sostojanii," *Kurs belorusovedenija*, Moscow, 1920. E. Karskij, Belorusy, vols. 1–2 (in 3 parts), Warsaw, 1903–12. G. Šerech, Problems in the formation of Belorussian, New York, 1954. C. Stang, Die westrussische Kanzleisprache des Grossfürstentums Litauen, Oslo, 1935. J. Stankevič, Mova rukapisu Al Kitab, Part I, New York, 1954. T. Lomtev, "Issledovanija v oblasti istorii belorusskogo sintaksisa," *Učen. zapiski Belorus. gos. universiteta, ser. filologičeskaja*, II, 1941.

Dictionaries

I. Nosovič, Slovar' belorusskogo narečija, St. Petersburg, 1870. M. Bajkov and S. Nekraševič, Belaruska-rasijski slovnik, Minsk, 1925. J. Kolas, Russko-belorusskij slovar', Moscow, 1953.

POLISH

Contemporary language

Z. Klemensiewicz, Podstawowe wiadomości z gramatyki języka polskiego, Cracow, 1952. H. Grappin, Grammaire de la langue polonaise, 2d ed., Paris, 1949. W. Doroszewski, Podstawy gramatyki polskiej, vol. 1, Warsaw, 1952. S. Szober, Gramatyka języka polskiego, vols. 1–2, Warsaw, 1931.

Sound pattern and morphology

H. Grappin, Introduction phonétique à l'étude de la langue polonaise, Paris, 1944. M. Dłuska, Fonetyka polska, vol. 1, Cracow, 1950. H. Koneczna and W. Zawadowski, Przekroje rentgenograficzne głosek polskich, Warsaw, 1951. Z. M. Arend, A Polish phonetic reader, London, 1921. A. Schenker, "Polish conjugation," *Word*, vol. 10, 1954.

Syntax

Z. Klemensiewicz, Zarys składni polskiej, Warsaw, 1953.

Dialectology

K. Nitsch, "Dialekty języka polskiego," *Gramatyka języka polskiego*, Cracow, 1923.

The language of American Poles

W. Doroszewski, Język polski w Stanach Zjednoczonych A.P., Warsaw, 1936.

History of Polish and other Lekhitic languages

T. Lehr-Spławiński, Język polski, pochodzenie, powstanie, rozwój, Warsaw, 1947. Z. Klemensiewicz, T. Lehr-Spławiński, and S. Urbańczyk, Gramatyka historyczna jezyka polskiego z dialektologią, Warsaw, 1955. J. Łoś, Gramatyka polska, vols. 1–3, Lwow, 1922–27. Z. Stieber, Rozwój fonologiczny języka polskiego, Warsaw, 1952. L. Bulaxovskij, Akcentologičeskij kommentarij k pol'skomu jazyku, Kiev, 1950.

History of literary Polish

S. Szober, Pochodzenie i rozwój polskiego języka literackiego, Warsaw, 1931.

Dictionaries of contemporary Polish

S. B. Linde, Słownik języka polskiego, vols. 1–6; reprint, Warsaw, 1952. A. Kryński, J. Karłowicz, and W. Niedźwiedzki, Słownik języka polskiego, vols. 1–8; reprint, Warsaw, 1952. S. Szober, Słownik ortoepiczny, Warsaw, 1937.

Dictionary of dialects

J. Karłowicz, Słownik gwar polskich, vols. 1–6, Cracow, 1900–11.

Historical dictionaries and lexical studies

A. Krasnowolski and W. Niedźwiedzki, Słownik staropolski, Warsaw, 1929. K. Nitsch (ed.), Słownik staropolski, Warsaw, from 1953. K. Nitsch, Studia z historii polskiego słownictwa, Cracow, 1948.

Etymological dictionaries

A. Brückner, Słownik etymologiczny języka polskiego, 2 vols., Cracow, 1927. F. Sławski, Słownik etymologiczny języka polskiego, Cracow, from 1952.

Guides and practical manuals in English

W. Kierst, Dictionary, English-Polish and Polish-English, London, 1946. M. Corbridge-Patkaniowska, Teach yourself Polish, New York, 1950.

Description and history

F. Lorentz, Gramatyka pomorska, Poznan, 1927–36. D. Bubrix, Severno-kašubskaja sistema udarenija, Leningrad, 1922. F. Lorentz, Geschichte der pomoranischen (kaschubischen) Sprache, Berlin, 1925.

Dictionaries

S. Ramułt, Słownik języka pomorskiego czyli kaszubskiego, Cracow, 1893. F. Lorentz, Slovinzisches Wörterbuch, vols. 1–2, St. Petersburg, 1908–12.

Guides and practical manuals in English

F. Lorentz, A. Fischer, and T. Lehr-Spławiński, The Cassubian civilization, London, 1935.

T. Lehr-Spławiński, Gramatyka połabska, Lwow, 1929. N. Trubetzkoy, Polabische Studien, Vienna, 1929. P. Rost, Die Sprachreste der Draväno-Polaben, Leipzig, 1907. J. Legowski and T. Lehr-Spławiński, "Szczątki języka dawnych słowiańskich mieszkańców wyspy Rugji," *Slavia occidentalis*, 2d vol., 1922. R. Trautmann, Die Elbe- und Ostseeslavischen Ortsnamen, Berlin, 1948. R. Trautmann, Die slavischen Ortsnamen Meklenburgs und Holsteins, Berlin, 1950.

Contemporary languages

B. Šẃela, Grammatik der niedersorbischen Sprache, Bautzen, 1952. P. Wowčerk, Kurzgefasste obersorbische Grammatik, Leipzig, 1951. P. Wirth, Beiträge zum sorbischen (wendischen) Sprachatlas, vols. 1–2, Leipzig, 1933–36. L. Ščerba, Vostočnolužickoe narečie, St. Petersburg, 1915.

Comparative history

Z. Stieber, Stosunki pokrewieństwa języków łużyckich, Cracow, 1934. G. Schwela, Vergleichende Grammatik der ober- und nieder-sorbischen Sprache, Bautzen, 1926. E. Mucke, Historische und vergleichende Laut- und Formenlehre der niedersorbischen Sprache, Leipzig, 1891.

Dictionaries

E. Muka, Słownik dolno-serbskeje rečy a jeje narečow, vols. 1–3, St. Petersburg-Prague, 1911–28. J. Kral, Serbsko-němski słownik hornjo-lužiskeje rěče, Bautzen, 1931.

Guides and practical manuals in English

G. Engerrand, The so-called Wends of Germany, Austin, 1934.

CZECH

Contemporary language

F. Trávníček, Mluvnice spisovné češtiny, vols. 1–2, Prague, 1948–49. V. Mathesius, Čeština a obecný jazykospyt, Prague, 1947.

Sound pattern

F. Trávníček, Úvod do české fonetiky, Prague, 1932. B. Polland and B. Hála, Artikulace českých zvuků v roentgenových obrazech, Prague, 1926. A. Frinta, A Czech phonetic reader, London, 1925.

Morphology

M. Vey, Morphologie du tchèque parlé, Paris, 1947. H. Rubenstein and J. Kučera, "Notes on the Czech conjugation," *Word*, vols. 7 and 8, 1951–52.

Syntax

V. Šmilauer, Novočeská skladba, Prague, 1947. F. Kopečný, Základy české skladby, Prague, 1952.

31

Dialectology

B. Havránek, "Nářečí česká," *Československá Vlastivěda*, vol. 3, Prague, 1934. T. Lehr-Spławiński, "Tło historyczne ugrupowania gwar czeskich," *Rocznik Slawistyczny*, vol. 17, 1952.

Comparative history of Czech and Slovak

O. Hujer, "Vývoj jazyka československého," *ČV*, vol. 3. F. Trávníček, Historická mluvnice československá, Prague, 1935. J. Gebauer, Historická mluvnice jazyka českého, vols. 1–4, Prague, 1894–1929. L. Bulaxovskij, Akcentologičeskij kommentarij k češskomu jazyku, Kiev, 1953.

History of literary Czech

B. Havránek, "Vývoj spisovného jazyka českého," *ČV*, supplementary vol., Prague, 1936.

Dictionaries of contemporary Czech

F. Trávníček, Slovník jazyka českého, 4th ed., Prague, 1952. Příruční slovník jazyka českého, published by the Czech Academy, from 1935.

Dialectological dictionary

F. Bartoš, Dialektologický slovník moravský, Prague, 1906.

Dictionaries of Old Czech

J. Gebauer, Slovník staročeský, 1st 2 vols., Prague, 1903–16. F. Šimek, Slovníček staré češtiny, Prague, 1947.

Etymological dictionary

J. Holub and F. Kopečný, Etymologický slovník jazyka českého, Prague, 1952.

Guides and practical manuals in English

A. Osička and I. Poldauf, Velký česko-anglický slovník, and Velký anglicko-český slovník, Prague, 1947 and 1948. W. Harkins, A modern Czech grammar, New York, 1953.

Contemporary language

J. Orlovský and L. Arany, Gramatika jazyka slovenského, Bratislava, 1946.

Sound pattern

B. Hála, Základy spisovné výslovnosti slovenské, Prague, 1929. L'. Novák, Fonologie a štúdium slovenčiny, Turč. Sv. Martin, 1934.

Morphology

E. Pauliny, Štruktura slovenského slovesa, Bratislava, 1943. E. Pauliny, Slovenské časovanie, Bratislava, 1949. B. Letz, Kmeňoslovné úvahy, Turč. Sv. Martin, 1943.

Dialectology

V. Vážný, "Nářečí slovenská," *ČV*, vol. 3.

History of literary Slovak

E. Pauliny, Dejiny spisovnej slovenčiny, Bratislava, 1948.

Early spread of Slovak

J. Stanislav, Slovenský juh v stredoveku, vols. 1–2 and maps, Turč. Sv. Martin, 1948.

Dictionaries

M. Kálal, Slovenský slovník z literatúry aj nárečí, Banská Bystrica, 1924. A. Jánošík and E. Jóna, Slovník spisovného jazyka slovenského, Turč. Sv. Martin, 1946.

Guides and practical manuals in English

J. J. Konuš, Slovak-English and English-Slovak dictionary, Pittsburgh, 1941. P. A. Hrobak, Slovak for beginners, Middletown, Pa., 1952.

Contemporary language

A. Breznik, Slovenska slovnica za srednje šole, Celje, 1934.

Sound pattern

F. Bezlaj, Oris slovenskega knjižnega izgovora, Ljubljana, 1939. M. Rupel, Slovensko pravorečje, Ljubljana, 1946.

Morphology

A. Bajec, Besedotvorje slovenskega jezika, vols. 1–2, Ljubljana, 1950–52.

Dialectology

F. Ramovš, Karta slovenskih narečij v priročni izdaji, Ljubljana, 1935.

History

F. Ramovš, Kratka zgodovina slovenskega jezika, vol. 1, Ljubljana, 1936. F. Ramovš, Historična gramatika slovenskega jezika, vols. 2 and 7, Ljubljana, 1924 and 1935. F. Ramovš, Morfologija slovenskega jezika, Ljubljana, 1952.

Dictionaries of contemporary Slovenian

M. Pleteršnik, Slovensko-nemški slovar, vols. 1–2, Ljubljana, 1894–95. J. Glonar, Slovar slovenskega jezika, Ljubljana, 1936.

Guides and practical manuals in English

F. Kotnik, Slovensko-angleski slovar, Ljubljana, 1952. R. Škerlj, Angleško-slovenski slovar, Ljubljana, 1952.

SERBOCROATIAN

Contemporary language

A. Belić, Savremeni srpskohrvatski jezik, 2 vols., Belgrade, 1949–51. A. Meillet and A. Vaillant, Grammaire de la langue serbocroate, 2d ed., Paris, 1952. M. Rešetar, Elementar-Grammatik der serbischen (kroatischen) Sprache, Zagreb, 1922. T. Maretić, Gramatika i stilistika hrvatskoga ili srpskoga književnog jezika, Zagreb, 1931.

Sound pattern

B. Miletić, Osnovi fonetike srpskog jezika, Belgrade, 1952.

Syntax

M. Lalević, Sintaksa srpskog jezika, Belgrade, 1951.

Dialectology

A. Belić, "Dialektologičeskaja karta serbskogo jazyka," Sbornik po slavjanovedeniju, 2d vol., St. Petersburg, 1905.

History of Serbocroatian

S. Kul'bakin, Serbskij jazyk, Kharkov, 1915. A. Leskien, Grammatik der serbokroatischen Sprache, vol. 1, Heidelberg, 1914.` A. Belić, Istorija srpskohrvatskog jezika, 2d vol. (2 issues), Belgrade, 1950–51.

History of literary Serbocroatian

F. Poljanec, Istorija srpskohrvatskog književnog jezika, Belgrade, 1931. B. Unbegaun, Les débuts de la langue littéraire chez les Serbes, Paris, 1935.

Dictionaries of contemporary Serbocroatian

Rječnik hrvatskoga ili srpskoga jezika, published by Jugoslavenska akademija, vols. 1–12, Zagreb, 1880–1914. V. Karadžić, Srpski rječnik, 4th ed., Belgrade, 1934.

Historical dictionary

B. Daničić, Rječnik iz književnih starina srpskih, vols. 1–3, Belgrade, 1863–64.

Guides and practical manuals in English

M. Drvodelić, Hrvatsko-engleski rječnik, Zagreb, 1953. I. M. Petrović, Praktičen englesko-srpski rečnik, Belgrade, 1951. J. D. Prince, Practical grammar of the Serbo-Croatian language; reprint, New York, 1945.

BULGARIAN

Contemporary language

L. Beaulieux, Grammaire de la langue bulgare, Paris, 1950. S. Mladenov, Gramatika na bъlgarskija ezik, Sofia, 1939. A. Teodorov-Balan, Nova bъlgarska gramatika, Sofia, 1940. L. Andrejčin, Osnovna bъlgarska gramatika, Sofia, 1944.

Sound pattern

S. Stojkov, Bъlgarski knižoven izgovor, Sofia, 1942.

Dialectology

L. Miletič, Das Ostbulgarische, Vienna, 1903. L. Miletič, Die Rhodopemundarten der bulgarischen Sprache, Vienna, 1912. S. Bernštejn, Razyskanija v oblasti bolgarskoj istoričeskoj dialektologii, vol. 1, Leningrad, 1948.

Comparative history of Bulgarian and Macedonian

K. Mirčev, Istorija na bълgarskija ezik, Sofia, 1950. S. Mladenov, Geschichte der bulgarischen Sprache, Berlin, 1929. B. Conev, Istorija na bълgarski ezik, vols. 1–4, Sofia, 1919–40.

Early spread of Bulgarian and other South Slavic dialects

M. Vasmer, Die Slaven in Griechenland, Berlin, 1941.

Dictionary of contemporary Bulgarian

N. Gerov, Rečnik na bълgarskija ezik, vols. 1–4, Plovdiv, 1895–1948.

Etymological dictionary

S. Mladenov, Etimologičeski i pravopisen rečnik na bългarskija knižoven ezik, Sofia, 1941.

Guides and practical manuals in English

R. Rusev, Bългаро-anglijski rečnik, Sofia, 1947. G. Čakalov, Anglo-bългarski rečnik, Sofia, 1947. S. Bernshtein, Short grammatical sketch of the Bulgarian language, Long Island City, 1952.

MACEDONIAN

Standard language

H. Lunt, Grammar of the Macedonian literary language, Skopje, 1952. B. Koneski, Gramatika na makedonskiot literaturen jazik, vols. 1–2, Skopje, 1952–54.

Dialectology

V. Oblak, Macedonische Studien, Vienna, 1896. A. Seliščev, Očerki po makedonskoj dialektologii, Kazan, 1918.

Bei Fragen zur Produktsicherheit wenden Sie sich bitte an:
If you have any questions regarding product safety,
please contact:

Walter de Gruyter GmbH
Genthiner Straße 13
10785 Berlin
productsafety@degruyterbrill.com